Spelling Three
An Interactive Vocabulary & Spelling Workbook for 7-Year-Olds.

(With AudioBook Lessons)

By
Bukky Ekine-Ogunlana

www.tcecpublishing.com

© Copyright Bukky Ekine-Ogunlana 2024 – All rights reserved.

The content of this book may not be reproduced, duplicated, or transmitted without direct written permission from the author or the publisher. Under no circumstance will any blame or legal responsibility be held against the publisher, or author, for any damages, reparation, or monetary loss due to the information contained within this book. Either directly or indirectly. You are responsible for your own choices, actions, and results.

Legal Notice:
This book is copyright protected. This book is only for personal use. You cannot amend, distribute, sell, use, quote, or paraphrase any part, or the content within this book, without the consent of the author or publisher.

Disclaimer Notice:
Please note the information contained within this document is for educational and entertainment purposes only. All effort has been executed to present accurate, up-to-date, reliable, and complete information. No warranties of any kind are declared or implied. Readers acknowledge that the author is not engaging in the rendering of legal, financial, medical, or professional advice. The content within this book has been derived from various sources. Please consult a licensed professional before attempting any techniques outlined in this book.

By reading this document, the reader agrees that under no circumstances is the author responsible for any direct or indirect losses incurred as a result of the use of the information contained within this document, including, but not limited to, errors, omissions, or inaccuracies.

Published by
TCEC Publishing

Table of Contents

Dedication 06
Introduction 07

Spelling 3-1 08
Spelling 3-2 12
Spelling 3-3 16
Spelling 3-4 20
Spelling 3-5 24
Spelling 3-6 28
Spelling 3-7 32
Spelling 3-8 36
Spelling 3-9 40
Spelling 3-10 44
Spelling 3-11 48
Spelling 3-12 52
Spelling 3-13 56
Spelling 3-14 60
Spelling 3-15 64
Spelling 3-16 68
Spelling 3-17 72
Spelling 3-18 76
Spelling 3-19 80
Spelling 3-20 84

Table of Contents

Spelling 3-21 88
Spelling 3-22 92
Spelling 3-23 96
Spelling 3-24 100
Spelling 3-25 104
Spelling 3-26 108
Spelling 3-27 112
Spelling 3-28 116
Spelling 3-29 120
Spelling 3-30 124
Spelling 3-31 128
Spelling 3-32 132
Spelling 3-33 136
Spelling 3-34 140
Spelling 3-35 144
Spelling 3-36 148

Conclusion 152
Answers 154
Other Books You Love 172
Audiobooks 176
Facebook Community 177
References 179

Dedication

This book is dedicated to our three exceptional children and all the beautiful children worldwide who have passed through the T.C.E.C 6-16 years program over the years. Thank you for the opportunity to serve you and invest in your colorful and bright future.

Introduction

Your spelling journey continues with the third book of the Spelling for Kids series.

Spelling 3 has another 432 words in store for you. As you can see, the number of words is rising with every chapter, as it is with your vocabulary and spelling performance! They go hand in hand. This book is ideal for 7-year-olds.

Listen to the dictation, Write, Check, and Repeat. That's the motto of your practice with every word. With this motto, you will master each word you learn in this chapter so you can proceed to the next one.

Remember that when you have finished Spelling 3, you will have known approximately 1,000 words! One thousand words plus in your vocabulary!

You are already walking the spelling road of excellence! Keep going to master it!

spelling 3-1

1. Spell:

Ben did _____ the ball.

2. Spell:

The football _____ is on Friday.

3. Spell:

I will attend Joshua's birthday party _____ he is my best friend.

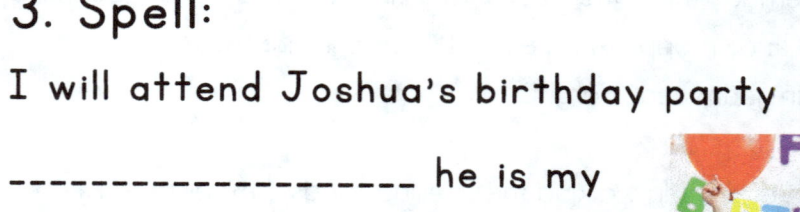

Spelling 3-1

4. Spell:

Hey Tom, have you _____ my pencil?

5. Spell:

Jake went to the hospital because of his

_____

temperature at school.

6. Spell:

Don't _____ at me like that! I am telling you the truth.

Spelling 3-1

7. Spell:
Hey! Did you see the monkey
_____ the tree?

8. Spell:
The plumber climbed on the
_____ to fix the
bathroom tap.

9. Spell:
Ella put the sliced apple in her
_____ .

Spelling 3-1

10. Spell:

Noah took a deep breath before the

_____ gave him

an injection.

11. Spell:

Shhh! Keep _____; the baby

is sleeping.

12. Spell:

David got more marks _____

his target grade.

Congrats! You have finished learning the words in lesson 1.

Spelling 3-2

1. Spell:

Jane will be playing with Connect 4 during _____ time.

2. Spell:

Tony can _____ playtime.

3. Spell:

The young family will be going on a _____ to California to see Mr. Martins.

Spelling 3-2

4. Spell:

The rat got into the set

_____.

5. Spell:

Mom, my _____ is aching.

Could we go to the dentist,

please?

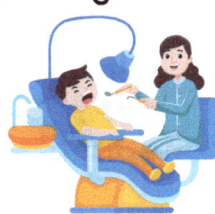

6. Spell:

I _____ it when dad changes

the channels on TV all the time.

Spelling 3-2

7. Spell:

I _____ doing my maths homework with my mum.

8. Spell:

There will be lots of food _____ the music rehearsal.

9. Spell:

Sheila wore a ring on her middle _____.

spelling 3-2

10. Spell:
I have _____ friends who care about me.

11. Spell:
My mum is always _____ doing lots of things at home.

12. Spell:
Mum, please can we buy that toy? It's on _____!

Great! You have finished learning the words in lesson 2.

Spelling 3-3

1. Spell:
Diana carried the _____ bag of rice to her grandmother.

2. Spell:
I like summer a lot and my best _____ is July. Why? Because I am going on vacation!

3. Spell:
Dorcas will _____ David off at school today.

Spelling 3-3

4. Spell:
Martina will _____ in the competition at her school.

5. Spell:
Stefan is the boy _____ our team's football success.

6. Spell:
Look how _____ this girl is, she has so many toys!

spelling 3-3

7. Spell:
Fishing is better when you do it from a
_____ .

8. Spell:
Zachary bought a new black
_____ for the new
academic year during the holiday.

9. Spell:
Kathy is separating the fight
_____ Rose
and Elizabeth.

Spelling 3-3

10. Spell:
Jessica got a _____ gift from her grandad on Sunday for completing all her spelling on time.

11. Spell:
The school bus was in a _____ to pick up the kids after school.

12. Spell:
We do not _____ from our classmates when we have an exam.

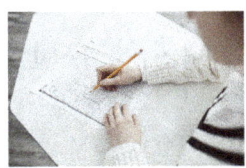

Great work! You have finished learning the words in lesson 3.

Spelling 3-4

1. Spell:
Oh, I love _____ Nancy because she always plays with me.

2. Spell:
My favorite meal is _____ with French fries.

3. Spell:
Reed _____ from Heathrow Airport in London to New York on Friday.

Spelling 3-4

4. Spell:

The team got _____ the expected grade.

5. Spell:

Look at these puppies; they are so _____ .

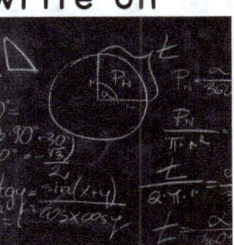

6. Spell:

I used _____ to write on the blackboard at playtime.

Spelling 3-4

7. Spell:
Mary, please _____ the door, because it's cold outside.

8. Spell:
We _____ all at Yvonne's house for the weekend.

9. Spell:
Sue was _____ in her room on Saturday.

Spelling 3-4

10. Spell:
Listening to _____ helps me to do my homework easier.

11. Spell:
Clive will _____ for his dance lesson when he has finished barbing his hair.

12. Spell:
Is Debby from the East _____ ?

Great! Lesson 4 is over! I suggest you get some rest before going on to the next lesson. That will help you recharge and return to the next task more refreshed! Great work!

Spelling 3-5

1. Spell:

There are many _____ in the playroom.

2. Spell:

Lucy went to sharpen her

_____ .

3. Spell:

Jack did _____ wrong.

Spelling 3-5

4. Spell:
Oops! I think I made a _____ in my spelling exam.

5. Spell:
It is _____ to eat candy without asking your mom first.

6. Spell:
Julia is a _____ 6-year-old girl.

Spelling 3-5

7. Spell:

Robert went to sit near the

_____

8. Spell:

Children! Next week you will have a

_____ in spelling, said the

teacher.

9. Spell:

Sean took a _____ to the

cinema with his dad.

Spelling 3-5

10. Spell:

Nick was sitting at the _____ of the table.

11. Spell:

Andy did not _____ at the joke.

12. Spell:

Keith's _____ won the game.

Fantastic! You have finished the words in lesson 5. What a task! Kids, keep a note: An easy way to learn the majority of new words is to break them apart; in that way, the words can be easily organised from the shortest to the longest.

Spelling 3-6

1. Spell:
I _____ I will go to the cinema with my dad this Saturday.

2. Spell:
Jessica will _____ her new toy at playtime.

3. Spell:
One _____ is twelve.

Spelling 3-6

4. Spell:

Leroy and Anna are _____

having their birthday on Friday.

5. Spell:

Leslie broke the _____ cup

by accident.

6. Spell:

I think our dog is hiding behind the

_____ .

Spelling 3-6

7. Spell:

Yvonne did her hair _____ at the new saloon.

8. Spell:

Stephen was the only _____ allowed to come and pick Daniel up after school.

9. Spell:

Besides our flat, we also have a country _____ by the lake.

Spelling 3-6

10. Spell:

Clive heard a loud _____

from his garden.

11. Spell:

Luke chose _____ instead of

false in the last question on the

test.

12. Spell:

Seeing you _____ all your

homework on time makes me

very proud of you!

Lesson 6 has come to an end. Awesome! Keep up the excellent work! And do not forget: Repetition makes the master!

Spelling 3-7

1. Spell:

Jake is Daniel's _____.

2. Spell:

The mechanic brought out the car

_____.

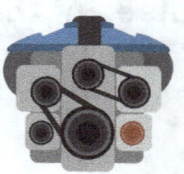

3. Spell:

Wow! Can you see how shiny her

_____ necklace

is?

Spelling 3-7

4. Spell:
Come on, kids! Wash your hands with _____ before sitting to eat lunch.

5. Spell:
James removed the _____ fly from his locker.

6. Spell:
Mathew was drawing a human _____ when he was bored.

Spelling 3-7

7. Spell:

Emma cut her vegetables with a sharp

_____.

8. Spell:

Hey Jim, don't _____ so fast! I can't reach you; please wait!

9. Spell:

Vanessa's mum will _____ her back after lunch.

spelling 3-7

10. Spell:
Michael is going to his drum _____ on Friday.

11. Spell:
Jenny, can you give me your phone _____ in case I have anything to ask you about today's lesson?

12. Spell:
Cody lives on the same _____ as Leah.

Look how far you have gone by now. You have reached and completed lesson 7! What a student you are! Congratulations!

Spelling 3-8

1. Spell:

_____ me! I know the road that leads to the hidden treasure.

2. Spell:

Two is an _____ number.

3. Spell:

Ben does not fight with _____.

Spelling 3-8

4. Spell:
This skirt is not your _____
Don't you see it does not fit you well?

5. Spell:
Ryan will _____ his drawing on the wall.

6. Spell:
The electrician came to fix the _____ that was cut.

Spelling 3-8

7. Spell:
Jackie's cat has a black _____ on its back.

8. Spell:
Leah will_____ her homework and hand it in on Tuesday.

9. Spell:
Ready? Say _____ so we can take you a photo smiling.

Spelling 3-8

10. Spell:
Come on, honey; _____ all of your orange juice. The school bus is waiting.

11. Spell:
Emmanuel will _____ the paper to draw a flower.

12. Spell:
Chris did _____ the bowl by accident.

Look at you! You are natural! And it seems that you will be a spelling bee master pretty soon! You have just finished lesson 8.

Spelling 3-9

1. Spell:
Rachel takes _____ many chocolates.

2. Spell:
The policeman did _____ straight.

3. Spell:
Mary _____ into her room crying loudly!

Spelling 3-9

4. Spell:

Nicky said the right _____ to the sad girl.

5. Spell:

Lexi and the _____ girls will fix the garden after play.

6. Spell:

My niece can draw a _____.

Spelling 3-9

7. Spell:

We _____ see the red bus on our way to school.

8. Spell:

My _____ Mark is also my son's best friend.

9. Spell:

Not every _____ in America has the same laws.

Spelling 3-9

10. Spell:

Mr. Clive was playing a _____ game.

11. Spell:

The incident did _____ on Monday.

12. Spell:

Mrs. Riley is a decent _____.

Well done! You have finished lesson 9. You should be proud of yourself! And remember this: Always enunciate each word properly; this method will help you spell the word correctly.

Spelling 3-10

1. Spell:

My _____ is having a party for grandpa and grandma.

2. Spell:

_____ are the cookies, mum? I want to eat some.

3. Spell:

I always drink a _____ of water every day.

Spelling 3-10

4. Spell:

Bethany will _____ her new dress for the party.

5. Spell:

Daniel wore a grey _____ for the interview.

6. Spell:

In school, we _____ many things.

Spelling 3-10

7. Spell:

My birthday is in the month of

_____.

8. Spell:

Michael bought a new _____ car for his wife.

9. Spell:

George has roast with _____ for dinner.

Spelling 3-10

10. Spell:

The headmaster played a

_____ in the class.

11. Spell:

One plus one adds up to _____.

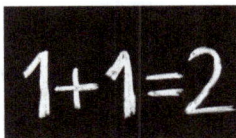

12. Spell:

My dad will _____ my room on Friday.

You completed lesson 10! Bravo! You are doing a great job. Pretty soon, you will be an expert in spelling.

Spelling 3-11

1. Spell:
Joshua's grandad is going to the _____ for his operation.

2. Spell:
Someday I will win the first _____ in a spelling contest!

3. Spell:
This spelling exercise is a _____ of cake for me!

Spelling 3-11

4. Spell:

The books are on the _____.

5. Spell:

The view from London _____

is spectacular; you can see

up to the Thames river.

6. Spell:

_____, mummy, can I watch

some more television? I am not

sleepy yet!

Spelling 3-11

7. Spell:

The _____ arrested the thief.

8. Spell:

Four _____ live in my house.

9. Spell:

Nathan stood _____ his dad in the photograph.

Spelling 3-11

10. Spell:

Lucy _____ her back when she was doing exercise at the gym.

11. Spell:

Mum, you don't need to _____, I have done my homework!

12. Spell:

Hey dad, I need some _____ with this exercise. Do you have a minute?

You have finished the words in lesson 11. Fantastic!

Spelling 3-12

1. Spell:
When is grandpa going to
_____ us?

2. Spell:
Jenny's mum taught her how to use the knife and _____ correctly.

3. Spell:
Grandma hurt her _____ at the field.

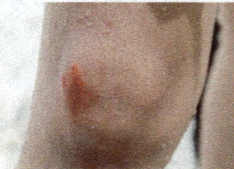

Spelling 3-12

4. Spell:
The secretary told the

_____ to sit down.

5. Spell:
John Dear, can you help me

_____ these

chairs from the kitchen?

6. Spell:
The hamburger is for the

_____ people

who did not come with us.

Spelling 3-12

7. Spell:
The news about the school nurse was a _____ to us.

8. Spell:
Tom added a pinch of _____ to his chips.

9. Spell:
Ever _____ I watched Cinderella, I have wanted to become a princess!

Spelling 3-12

10. Spell:

Joseph had a _____ slice of cake at the party.

11. Spell:

The clown did _____ everyone up.

12. Spell:

The _____ hall was closed.

> You have done a great job finishing words in lesson 12. With this rhythm, you are about to be a master in spelling soon.

Spelling 3-13

1. Spell:
To catch the first train tomorrow, we should get up _____ .

2. Spell:
Santa Claus brought me my favorite doll as a _____ this Christmas!

3. Spell:
Ben was _____ to hold the spider.

Spelling 3-13

4. Spell:
I am happy because I _____ all the words in this spelling test!

5. Spell:
Every driver should have a _____ in their car in case the GPS doesn't work!

6. Spell:
Kate gave the baby a friendly _____ .

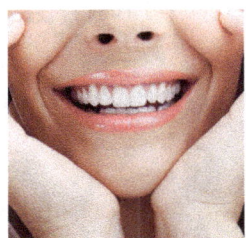

Spelling 3-13

7. Spell:

The new whiteboard is at the

_____ of the class.

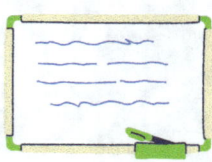

8. Spell:

Spiderman's _____ is magical

and helps him climb the buildings!

9. Spell:

David will _____ the candle

in the night.

spelling 3-13

10. Spell:

One _____ is twelve.

11. Spell:

The _____ was at the hospital to do his work.

12. Spell:

The class _____ will be emailed home to parents.

Congrats! You have made such Progress! You finished the words in lesson 13 already. Don't forget to practice new vocabulary every week. First, learn the meaning of the word, and the spelling of it. Then surprise everyone with your spelling skills.

Spelling 3-14

1. Spell:
Betty was full of _____ on the wedding occasion.

2. Spell:
My grandpa prefers listening to the _____ than watching TV.

3. Spell:
Four is _____ than ten.

Spelling 3-14

4. Spell:

I will _____ my food until I am ready to eat it.

5. Spell:

I am so _____ I passed the spelling test without mistakes.

6. Spell:

I wish you a _____ Christmas.

spelling 3-14

7. Spell:

The cat did _____ the dog.

8. Spell:

My mother always prepares me

_____ for school.

9. Spell:

Did you see that_____ ? It looked like it tore the sky in two parts!

Spelling 3-14

10. Spell:

_____ the teacher was right.

11. Spell:

Shaking the _____ makes my baby sister giggle.

12. Spell:

Mum, I'm so _____ ! What do we have for dinner?

What progress! You completed lesson 14 already. You should be proud of yourself!

spelling 3-15

1. Spell:

I take one teaspoon of

_____ with my oat.

2. Spell:

Ben and his sister do suck their

_____.

3. Spell:

When I help mum make biscuits with my

sister, we play with the

_____ and

spread it all over the table!

Spelling 3-15

4. Spell:
When grandpa was _____, he traveled a lot to the whole world.

5. Spell:
The car can seat four _____ .

6. Spell:
Growing up, I want to serve my _____ in the military.

Spelling 3-15

7. Spell:

I can _____ why my grandma said she would come with me.

8. Spell:

Kitty was in _____ at school.

9. Spell:

The sick _____ could not eat up his bananas.

Spelling 3-15

10. Spell:
There was a _____ in the plane's arrival, so we had to wait for 2 hours at the airport.

11. Spell:
The class teacher will give the end-of-year _____ today.

12. Spell:
My mum wants me to take a nap in the _____ .

Wonderful! You have completed words in lesson 15. Keep up the excellent work, and don't forget: Words matter, and most importantly, correctly written words matter.

Spelling 3-16

1. Spell:

The toilet _____ has finished.

2. Spell:

We should always _____ on the door before we enter a room.

3. Spell:

Jude _____ the glass cup.

Spelling 3-16

4. Spell:

It was a big _____ to get my brother to do his homework.

5. Spell:

I _____ sad when our kitten got sick.

6. Spell:

_____ to your dad Mike, and turn off the TV, said mum.

Spelling 3-16

7. Spell:

I enjoy going to the _____

with my parents.

8. Spell:

I always write the short

_____ at school.

9. Spell:

I _____ travel alone.

Spelling 3-16

10. Spell:
The princess kissed the frog, and he
_____ a prince!

11. Spell:
We can see some _____
animals at the zoo, like lions
and tigers.

12. Spell:
_____ is the color that
comes from mixing white and
black color.

You're almost finished with becoming a spelling master. You are doing so well! You have completed words in spelling lesson 16. Bravo!

Spelling 3-17

1. Spell:
The Captain _____ the plane for 8 hours.

2. Spell:
Daniel has _____ failing his writing test.

3. Spell:
My parents keep all the bills in a _____ .

Spelling 3-17

4. Spell:

"Tom and Jerry" are such

_____ cartoons.

5. Spell:

My aunt brought me a present in a fancy

_____ with a big

ribbon!

6. Spell:

The opposite of the _____

is the north.

spelling 3-17

7. Spell:
I have _____ one daddy.

8. Spell:
My mum gave a penny to the _____ old man outside the church.

9. Spell:
Okay, children, _____ down your name before you begin the test, said the teacher.

Spelling 3-17

10. Spell:

The _____ was too slow for me.

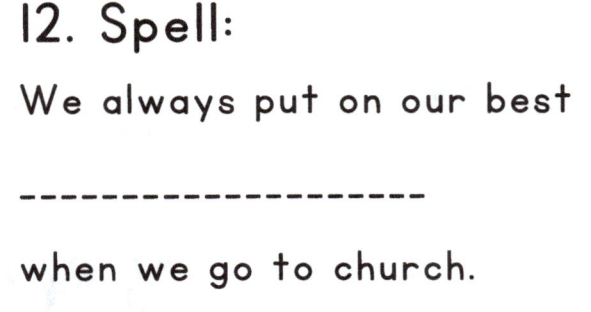

11. Spell:

George's best _____ is netball.

12. Spell:

We always put on our best _____ when we go to church.

Fantastic! You have completed spelling lesson 17! You're almost done. Don't quit now! You are close to the end.

Spelling 3-18

1. Spell:
The wind blew up the new

_____.

2. Spell:
During the winter, my mum always wears a

_____ when she goes

out.

3. Spell:
The brown cat sat _____ the

mat and fell asleep.

Spelling 3-18

4. Spell:
She invited _____ sister to the training.

5. Spell:
Mary cut her _____ short, and now she looks like a boy.

6. Spell:
A sharp _____ can cut the meat.

Spelling 3-18

7. Spell:
Jude wants to be a _____ when he grows up because he likes the sea very much.

8. Spell:
Kelly saves every _____ she gets.

9. Spell:
We should always tell the _____ to mum and dad and not hide anything from them.

Spelling 3-18

10. Spell:
Dad is always _____ after working out at the gym.

11. Spell:
Nina had a _____ of coco pops for breakfast.

12. Spell:
When I grow up, I will have my own _____ to buy my parents presents.

Spelling lesson 18 is over. You finished it and, more importantly, learned the lesson's words. However, if you have doubts about one or more words, do not worry; return to the address and make as many revisions as necessary.

Spelling 3-19

1. Spell:
"Beauty and the Beast" is my favorite _____ tale.

2. Spell:
He is cheerful in _____ of his losing the game.

3. Spell:
The wound on Jonathan's leg will take some time to _____.

Spelling 3-19

4. Spell:
My big brother was _____ with his predictions.

5. Spell:
_____ is made from bees.

6. Spell:
Mary and Helen are going to the _____ on Saturday.

Spelling 3-19

7. Spell:
I don't _____ dancing in public.

8. Spell:
The birthday _____ will start at noon. Is the birthday cake ready?

9. Spell:
The older man has lost his _____.

Spelling 3-19

10. Spell:

We should protect planet

_____ because it is

our home.

11. Spell:

Bob was standing at the

_____ gate.

12. Spell:

My mummy makes me kitchen

_____ when I have

the flu.

You have done excellent job finishing words in lesson 19.

Spelling 3-20

1. Spell:
Daniel touched the _____ on David's head.

2. Spell:
The baby could not _____ because of the noise.

3. Spell:
Zorro was famous for wearing a black mask and a black _____.

Spelling 3-20

4. Spell:
The monkey climbed up the
_____ and ate the
banana.

5. Spell:
The boys in my class are
_____.

6. Spell:
Daniel said _____
to his dad.

Spelling 3-20

7. Spell:

Lily keeps her needles and thread in her sewing _____.

8. Spell:

"Go _____ Tom," said mum, "it's snowing, and you will catch a cold."

9. Spell:

Nathan did not _____ his eight-times- table during the test.

Spelling 3-20

10. Spell:

_____! And suddenly the bright lights were on and the birthday cake appeared!

11. Spell:

Now that all the family is here, we can take a _____ to remember.

12. Spell:

Billy threw the plastic cup away because it was not _____.

You have finished the words in lesson 20 Fantastic!

Spelling 3-21

1. Spell:
A _____ noise came from the basement. Was that the cat?

2. Spell:
The _____ is a kind driver.

3. Spell:
Teddy's _____ was loud in class today.

Spelling 3-21

4. Spell:

Two is an even _____.

5. Spell:

Washing your teeth _____ a day keeps them clean and healthy!

6. Spell:

Kate was able to _____ the new baby.

Spelling 3-21

7. Spell:

_____ my words son, if you study every day for 10 minutes, by summer, you will be the best speller!

8. Spell:

Sue had to _____ the image to fit into the frame.

9. Spell:

Dan is too _____ with his exercise.

Spelling 3-21

10. Spell:
When we give a promise, we should not _____ it.

11. Spell:
Billy is a _____ boy to have carried the table alone.

12. Spell:
The old lady planted a new _____ in her garden.

What progress! You have completed lesson 14.

Spelling 3-22

1. Spell:

Helen knew that her daughter was in _____.

2. Spell:

The goalkeeper _____ the ball.

3. Spell:

Ben has _____ of money in his money bag.

Spelling 3-22

4. Spell:

David and his brother had coco pops for their _____ today.

5. Spell:

The _____ looks good today, so I will not need my umbrella.

6. Spell:

The doctor said my gran is in good

_____.

Spelling 3-22

7. Spell:
Billy made a new _____ today at the playground.

8. Spell:
The old lady lives on the _____ floor.

9. Spell:
We drew a _____ in the art class today.

Spelling 3-22

10. Spell:

Rita and Rose are from the same

_____.

11. Spell:

Ted was really _____ with all his birthday gifts and opened them immediately.

12. Spell:

Tim _____ his right foot on the playground.

Wonderful! You have completed words in lesson 22.

Spelling 3-23

1. Spell:
Jude was feeling the _____ of the sun on his back.

2. Spell:
Simba, the Lion King, stood in the mountain and looked down the _____.

3. Spell:
The test was _____ for everyone, and all scored high marks.

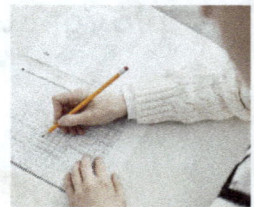

Spelling 3-23

4. Spell:

Do you want _____ topping on your ice cream?

5. Spell:

Let's play connect 4 _____ of a monopoly.

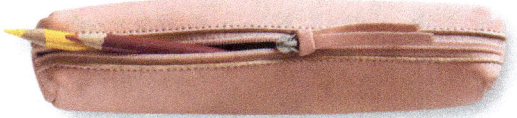

6. Spell:

The pencil case is _____ in my room.

Spelling 3-23

7. Spell:
I looked _____ for my phone, but I could not find it.

8. Spell:
_____ better at spelling means you have to study every day.

9. Spell:
Ben's boat approached a small _____.

Spelling 3-23

10. Spell:
The family had a _____ to deal with.

11. Spell:
_____ came for the swimming lesson because it was raining.

12. Spell:
Danny will _____ the whole class to his birthday party.

Well done! You have finished lesson 23.

Spelling 3-24

1. Spell:
Debby always looks _____, no matter what she wears.

2. Spell:
The gardener was _____ a minute ago.

3. Spell:
The _____ boy cried through the night.

Spelling 3-24

4. Spell:

I cannot choose _____

Spiderman and Batman because

I like them both.

5. Spell:

_____ left the window open,

and the rain entered

the living room.

6. Spell:

The _____ is wide and clean.

Spelling 3-24

7. Spell:
Don't you ever touch the _____ with wet hands!

8. Spell:
I heard a _____ noise in the car.

9. Spell:
One _____ is sixty minutes.

Spelling 3-24

10. Spell:

You can _____ your goal in life when you work hard.

11. Spell:

Do you _____ the name of Simba in the Lion King movie? Yes, it was King Mufasa.

12. Spell:

The weekend was _____ with lots of activities.

Well done! You have finished lesson 24. You should be proud of yourself!

Spelling 3-25

1. Spell:

Tony gave her a _____ of cake.

2. Spell:

_____ bag is this?

3. Spell:

_____ you should tell your mother about this.

Spelling 3-25

4. Spell:
Dad loves homemade _____ salad.

5. Spell:
Billy sliced the _____ and put it in the pan with the omelet.

6. Spell:
Jude is a true friend _____.

Spelling 3-25

7. Spell:
No _____ on earth should suffer from starvation.

8. Spell:
Singapore has one of the biggest _____ in the world.

9. Spell:
Ken did not water the _____, so it died.

Spelling 3-25

10. Spell:

Ani sat at the _____ of the staircase when she was sad.

11. Spell:

The electricity bill is due to be paid in _____.

12. Spell:

Should I make you a _____ salad while you do your spelling exercises, sweetie?

Well done! You have finished lesson 25.

Spelling 3-26

1. Spell:

Paul saw a _____ spider in his wardrobe.

2. Spell:

Do not _____ the wire next to the computer.

3. Spell:

I _____ all the school rules and class rules.

Spelling 3-26

4. Spell:
January is the first calendar _____ of the year.

5. Spell:
The _____ ate the little Red Riding Hood's grandma and dressed like her.

6. Spell:
The _____ man used to be one of my favorite heroes.

Spelling 3-26

7. Spell:
What's so _____ about it, and you can't stop laughing?

8. Spell:
You are making _____ progress in your spelling.

9. Spell:
There was calmness after the _____.

Spelling 3-26

10. Spell:

Are you on _____ with your spelling?

11. Spell:

_____ of my classmates have smartphones already.

12. Spell:

Here, _____ some ice cream. It's homemade.

Well done! You have finished lesson 26. You should be proud of yourself!

Spelling 3-27

1. Spell:
Before I go to bed, my mummy always brings me a _____ cup of milk to drink.

2. Spell:
The _____ King remains my favorite movie.

3. Spell:
My mommy made me a smoothie with milk, banana, apple, and _____.

Spelling 3-27

4. Spell:
We can leave for vacation now;
_____ is set.

5. Spell:
They walked _____ the path quietly.

6. Spell:
I _____ pray with my family before I go to bed.

Spelling 3-27

7. Spell:
The coach will _____ the team equally.

8. Spell:
The timetable is _____ to me.

9. Spell:
Sonny's _____ feels dry.

Spelling 3-27

10. Spell:
There was a fatal _____ on the main road last night.

11. Spell:
Billy _____ splits the milk on the floor.

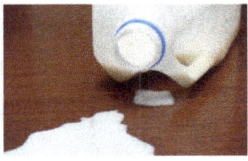

12. Spell:
The _____ price will not be displayed on the notice board.

You completed lesson 27

Spelling 3-28

1. Spell:
We _____ made the class teacher proud by singing well in the assembly.

2. Spell:
The house _____ has changed since we moved house to another city.

3. Spell:
_____ I wear the school uniform, I do not like it.

Spelling 3-28

4. Spell:

Sheila did not know the

_____ to the

first question.

5. Spell:

Dan was asked to _____ on a

television show.

6. Spell:

The school bus will _____ on

time.

Spelling 3-28

7. Spell:
Why don't you _____ me when I told you I did my homework, mum?

8. Spell:
Lilian rode her_____ to school.

9. Spell:
Tina took a deep _____ before the nurse gave her an injection.

Spelling 3-28

10. Spell:
When I visit my village, I _____ fresh air.

11. Spell:
The team will _____ a Lego car tomorrow.

12. Spell:
The week has been _____ for everyone.

You completed lesson 28! You are doing a great job.

Spelling 3-29

1. Spell:
I always mind my _____ .

2. Spell:
I check today's date in a

_____

3. Spell:
Jenny _____ a cold because she went out without wearing her coat.

Spelling 3-29

4. Spell:
The class was sitting at the
_____ of the
field after the match.

5. Spell:
During the previous _____ ,
people did not have cell phones.

6. Spell:
No one is _____ about the
school trip in the summer.

Spelling 3-29

7. Spell:

Daniel did _____ his task faster than Jude.

8. Spell:

I _____ my dad my best friend.

9. Spell:

She will _____ her spelling tomorrow.

Spelling 3-29

10. Spell:

I cannot _____ which one I like the most; vanilla or chocolate ice cream.

11. Spell:

Can you _____ to me what you saw in the circus?

12. Spell:

There are _____ games available in the school.

Bravo! You are doing a great job.

Spelling 3-30

1. Spell:
I sometimes find maths_____ to understand, but I do the sums quickly.

2. Spell:
I searched all my room, and I have not found my red pencil! Did it _____ from the earth?

3. Spell:
There are _____ pencils in the pencil case.

Spelling 3-30

4. Spell:

Jane was the _____ person who scored a hundred percent in the exams.

5. Spell:

_____ is _____ !This behavior unacceptable, and I will not   tolerate it anymore!

6. Spell:

I always follow my _____ routine to stay fit.

Spelling 3-30

7. Spell:
Mr. Davies has over ten years of _____ driving a lorry.

8. Spell:
We usually _____ every day in chemistry lessons to understand how materials react.

9. Spell:
The team talked about _____ topics.

Spelling 3-30

10. Spell:

Lisa was in _____ pain, so she went to the nurse.

11. Spell:

Danny has become _____ for his music.

12. Spell:

Joseph's _____ food is chicken and chips with peas.

You completed lesson 30! Well done! You are doing a great job.

Spelling 3-31

1. Spell:
By _____ , I will have learned half of the words in my spelling book.

2. Spell:
We all look _____ to a snowy Christmas in December.

3. Spell:
The bus driver stopped unexpectedly, and the passengers were jolted _____ .

Spelling 3-31

4. Spell:
Apple is the best _____ .

5. Spell:
Knowing _____ is essential for speaking and writing correctly.

6. Spell:
Mr. Smith split the _____ into four because there were too many people.

Spelling 3-31

7. Spell:
David's uncle is the security _____ at the shopping mall.

8. Spell:
Let's look at the museum's _____ to learn more about this statue.

9. Spell:
The baby shivered when she _____ the loud noise from the road.

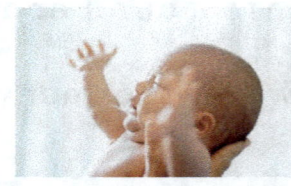

Spelling 3-31

10. Spell:
Somehow I knew that what he said to me came from his _____, which was true.

11. Spell:
Joshua is not afraid of _____ anymore after he came back from Australia.

12. Spell:
_____ repeats itself.

You completed lesson 31! Bravo! You are doing a great job.

Spelling 3-32

1. Spell:

I can _____ what the world will be like in a hundred years.

2. Spell:

There seems to be an _____ in the world's population.

3. Spell:

It is _____ you remember the methods used in the class to solve the problems.

Spelling 3-32

4. Spell:

Felix has demonstrated a genuine

_____ in science

and maths

5. Spell:

Felix needs to gain more

_____ in geography.

6. Spell:

Hey, Sam! Did you _____ all

the words in today's exercise?

Spelling 3-32

7. Spell:
The _____ of this swimming pool is three meters long.

8. Spell:
Betty went to borrow some books at the _____

9. Spell:
The _____ she used for making her clothes was not enough, so she bought some more.

Spelling 3-32

10. Spell:
The old lady takes her _____ with water.

11. Spell:
The teacher will _____ what happened in the class to my parents.

12. Spell:
Hey, wait a _____ ! I am not ready yet!

Lesson 32 has come to an end. Awesome! Keep up the excellent work!

Spelling 3-33

1. Spell:
Bella has some _____ abilities.

2. Spell:
Please take _____ of this sign. Only adults can watch this TV series.

3. Spell:
You will not be allowed a time out on this _____

Spelling 3-33

4. Spell:

Only _____ am I allowed to play with my tablet.

5. Spell:

I _____ see my mentor when I am in Japan.

6. Spell:

The car went in the _____ direction from the one that I showed the driver.

Spelling 3-33

7. Spell:

An _____ girl, Katy, drew a fantastic flower for the art competition.

8. Spell:

My mummy is _____ about the school I go to next year.

9. Spell:

There is something _____ about her likable character.

Spelling 3-33

10. Spell:

A _____ footballer is coming to our school to train the children.

11. Spell:

Mark was being naughty and brought his mother into an awkward _____ .

12. Spell:

How many bags do you _____ ?

Fantastic! You have completed spelling lesson 33! You're almost done.

Spelling 3-34

1. Spell:
Mr. Ali lost all his _____ during the Ukraine war.

2. Spell:
There is only one _____ answer for that particular question the teacher asked.

3. Spell:
We have roast _____ for dinner every Sunday.

Spelling 3-34

4. Spell:

The nurse came to measure her blood _____ because she was not feeling well.

5. Spell:

Tom _____ won't come to the party, because he was sick.

6. Spell:

He did _____ to behave better in the next class.

Spelling 3-34

7. Spell:
We need to have a _____ in life to live it to the fullest.

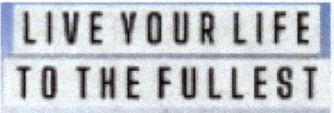

8. Spell:
A _____ of eight is two.

9. Spell:
Does anyone have a _____ to ask about today's lesson? Asked the teacher.

Spelling 3-34

10. Spell:
Dad brought me a camera from his _____ trip to California.

11. Spell:
Can I please have a milkshake in the _____ size?

12. Spell:
The king will _____ for some more years.

Spelling lesson 34 is over. You finished it and, more importantly, learned the lesson's words. However, if you have doubts about one or more words, do not worry; return to the word and make as many revisions as necessary.

Spelling 3-35

1. Spell:
I did not _____ to take my lunch box to school.

2. Spell:
Each _____ includes a word you must learn to spell correctly.

3. Spell:
The teacher had to _____ James and Joshua because they were distracting in the lesson.

Spelling 3-35

4. Spell:
I wear my favorite dress on _____ occasions.

5. Spell:
I can draw a _____ line with a ruler.

6. Spell:
Freddie's idea of solving the problem was new and _____ .

Spelling 3-35

7. Spell:

The old lady did not have enough

_____ to stand up,

so she was asked to sit down.

8. Spell:

_____ you forgot the key to

the house; what would you do?

9. Spell:

Helen got a doll's house as a

_____ birthday

gift.

Spelling 3-35

10. Spell:
The scooter is broken;_____,
I cannot ride it.

11. Spell:
My _____ is with Tom now that he has lost his grandpa.

12. Spell:
_____ it is night time, I can still see.

Excellent work, kid! You have made it! You are so lose to the end. Lesson 35 is complete. One more task is left, and you are done. Right? Okay, let's go!

Spelling 3-36

1. Spell:
The _____ in the dining hall were all friendly and kind.

2. Spell:
I like to take my snowboard and _____ smoothly down the snowy hill.

3. Spell:
He _____ his arms as he walks on the road.

Spelling 3-36

4. Spell:
I must _____ that Tom, despite his absence, remains an excellent student, said the teacher.

5. Spell:
I _____ not having told you the truth from the start.

6. Spell:
This is private _____, and access is denied!

spelling 3-36

7. Spell:
Tom's _____ has gone down to 10 kilograms.

8. Spell:
What a _____ boy! His mom asked him to behave at least five times!

9. Spell:
We had to _____ our names on the computer.

Spelling 3-36

10. Spell:
The _____ went away after a good sleep.

11. Spell:
After taking aspirin, my _____ passed.

12. Spell:
The lady _____ her baby when crying because she was on her phone.

> Here we are! Last lesson, and you have reached the end of Spelling 3. Do you feel like you have conquered the vocabulary and spelling word? Great! You should be proud of yourself. If, however, you do not feel very confident with some of the words, repeat them again and again until you fully understand the meaning and the orthography.

Conclusion

Congratulations! You are the star of spelling!

You have finally reached the end of Spelling 3!

And you deserve to celebrate it. After all, you have just learned 432 new words by finishing this book. And you are one step closer to gaining the spelling medal. So, let's toast your spelling journey and your dedication!

One thing to remember though: Don't forget that making regular revisions on the words you got wrong preferably about five times each can ensure your ticket to a seat next to the champions of correct dictation.

Next challenge ahead: Spelling 4 is waiting for you.
Are you ready to conquer new words?

I'll meet you there

Please leave a 1-click Review!

I would be incredibly thankful if you could take just 60 seconds to write a brief review on Amazon or the platform of purchase, even if it's just a few sentences!

Answers

Spelling 3-1

1. Spell: <u>Catch</u>
2. Spell: <u>Match</u>
3. Spell: <u>Because</u>
4. Spell: <u>Seen</u>
5. Spell: <u>High</u>
6. Spell: <u>Stare</u>
7. Spell: <u>Climb</u>
8. Spell: <u>Ladder</u>
9. Spell: <u>Mouth</u>
10. Spell: <u>Nurse</u>
11. Spell: <u>Quiet</u>
12. Spell: <u>Above</u>

Spelling 3-2

1. Spell: <u>Break</u>
2. Spell: <u>Skip</u>
3. Spell: <u>Trip</u>
4. Spell: <u>Trap</u>
5. Spell: <u>Tooth</u>
6. Spell: <u>Hate</u>
7. Spell: <u>Enjoy</u>
8. Spell: <u>During</u>
9. Spell: <u>Finger</u>
10. Spell: <u>Few</u>
11. Spell: <u>Busy</u>
12. Spell: <u>Sale</u>

Answers

Spelling 3-3

1. Spell: Heavy
2. Spell: Month
3. Spell: Drop
4. Spell: Swim
5. Spell: Behind
6. Spell: Rich
7. Spell: Boat
8. Spell: Coat
9. Spell: Between
10. Spell: Surprise
11. Spell: Hurry
12. Spell: Copy

Spelling 3-4

1. Spell: Aunt
2. Spell: Beef
3. Spell: Flew
4. Spell: Below
5. Spell: Tiny
6. Spell: Chalk
7. Spell: Close
8. Spell: Were
9. Spell: Alone
10. Spell: Music
11. Spell: Leave
12. Spell: Coast

Answers

Spelling 3-5

1. Spell: Babies
2. Spell: Pencil
3. Spell: Nothing
4. Spell: Mistake
5. Spell: Wrong
6. Spell: Young
7. Spell: Ocean
8. Spell: Test
9. Spell: Taxi
10. Spell: Edge
11. Spell: Laugh
12. Spell: Team

Spelling 3-6

1. Spell: Hope
2. Spell: Share
3. Spell: Dozen
4. Spell: Both
5. Spell: Glass
6. Spell: Bush
7. Spell: Once
8. Spell: Person
9. Spell: House
10. Spell: Noise
11. Spell: True
12. Spell: Finish

Answers

Spelling 3-7

1. Spell: Uncle
2. Spell: Engine
3. Spell: Silver
4. Spell: Soap
5. Spell: Dead
6. Spell: Body
7. Spell: Knife
8. Spell: Run
9. Spell: Rub
10. Spell: Lesson
11. Spell: Number
12. Spell: Street

Spelling 3-8

1. Spell: Follow
2. Spell: Even
3. Spell: Anyone
4. Spell: Size
5. Spell: Paste
6. Spell: Wire
7. Spell: Patch
8. Spell: Print
9. Spell: Cheese
10. Spell: Drink
11. Spell: Use
12. Spell: Smash

Answers

Spelling 3-9

1. Spell: Too
2. Spell: Shoot
3. Spell: Burst
4. Spell: Word
5. Spell: Other
6. Spell: River
7. Spell: Sometimes
8. Spell: Nephew
9. Spell: State
10. Spell: Rough
11. Spell: Happen
12. Spell: Lady

Spelling 3-10

1. Spell: Family
2. Spell: Where
3. Spell: Bottle
4. Spell: Wear
5. Spell: Suit
6. Spell: Learn
7. Spell: March
8. Spell: Motor
9. Spell: Lamb
10. Spell: Trick
11. Spell: Two
12. Spell: Paint

Answers

Spelling 3-11

1. Spell: Hospital
2. Spell: Prize
3. Spell: Piece
4. Spell: Shelf
5. Spell: Bridge
6. Spell: Please
7. Spell: Police
8. Spell: People
9. Spell: Behind
10. Spell: Hurt
11. Spell: Worry
12. Spell: Help

Spelling 3-12

1. Spell: Visit
2. Spell: Fork
3. Spell: Knee
4. Spell: Woman
5. Spell: Move
6. Spell: Other
7. Spell: Shock
8. Spell: Salt
9. Spell: Since
10. Spell: Thin
11. Spell: Cheer
12. Spell: Dance

Answers

Spelling 3-13

1. Spell: <u>Early</u>
2. Spell: <u>Present</u>
3. Spell: <u>Brave</u>
4. Spell: <u>Know</u>
5. Spell: <u>Map</u>
6. Spell: <u>Smile</u>
7. Spell: <u>Front</u>
8. Spell: <u>Glove</u>
9. Spell: <u>Light</u>
10. Spell: <u>Dozen</u>
11. Spell: <u>Doctor</u>
12. Spell: <u>Report</u>

Spelling 3-14

1. Spell: <u>Life</u>
2. Spell: <u>Radio</u>
3. Spell: <u>Less</u>
4. Spell: <u>Cover</u>
5. Spell: <u>Happy</u>
6. Spell: <u>Merry</u>
7. Spell: <u>Chase</u>
8. Spell: <u>Lunch</u>
9. Spell: <u>Thunder</u>
10. Spell: <u>Perhaps</u>
11. Spell: <u>Rattle</u>
12. Spell: <u>Hungry</u>

Answers

Spelling 3-15

1. Spell: Sugar
2. Spell: Thumb
3. Spell: Flour
4. Spell: Young
5. Spell: People
6. Spell: Country
7. Spell: Understand
8. Spell: Trouble
9. Spell: Monkey
10. Spell: Delay
11. Spell: Report
12. Spell: Afternoon

Spelling 3-16

1. Spell: Paper
2. Spell: Knock
3. Spell: Broke
4. Spell: Battle
5. Spell: Was
6. Spell: Listen
7. Spell: Market
8. Spell: Date
9. Spell: Cannot
10. Spell: Became
11. Spell: Wild
12. Spell: Grey

Answers

Spelling 3-17

1. Spell: Flew
2. Spell: Dreaded
3. Spell: File
4. Spell: Funny
5. Spell: Box
6. Spell: South
7. Spell: Only
8. Spell: Poor
9. Spell: Write
10. Spell: Speed
11. Spell: Sport
12. Spell: Clothes

Spelling 3-18

1. Spell: Fence
2. Spell: Scarf
3. Spell: On
4. Spell: Her
5. Spell: Hair
6. Spell: Knife
7. Spell: Sailor
8. Spell: Cent
9. Spell: Truth
10. Spell: Thirsty
11. Spell: Bowl
12. Spell: Money

Answers

Spelling 3-19

1. Spell: <u>Fairy</u>
2. Spell: <u>Spite</u>
3. Spell: <u>Heal</u>
4. Spell: <u>Right</u>
5. Spell: <u>Honey</u>
6. Spell: <u>Store</u>
7. Spell: <u>Enjoy</u>
8. Spell: <u>Party</u>
9. Spell: <u>Sight</u>
10. Spell: <u>Earth</u>
11. Spell: <u>North</u>
12. Spell: <u>Soup</u>

Spelling 3-20

1. Spell: <u>Bump</u>
2. Spell: <u>Sleep</u>
3. Spell: <u>Cloak</u>
4. Spell: <u>Tree</u>
5. Spell: <u>Smart</u>
6. Spell: <u>Goodbye</u>
7. Spell: <u>Pouch</u>
8. Spell: <u>Inside</u>
9. Spell: <u>Remember</u>
10. Spell: <u>Surprise</u>
11. Spell: <u>Picture</u>
12. Spell: <u>Useful</u>

Answers

Spelling 3-21

1. Spell: <u>Strange</u>
2. Spell: <u>Woman</u>
3. Spell: <u>Voice</u>
4. Spell: <u>Number</u>
5. Spell: <u>Twice</u>
6. Spell: <u>Carry</u>
7. Spell: <u>Mark</u>
8. Spell: <u>Crop</u>
9. Spell: <u>Slow</u>
10. Spell: <u>Break</u>
11. Spell: <u>Strong</u>
12. Spell: <u>Flower</u>

Spelling 3-22

1. Spell: <u>Danger</u>
2. Spell: <u>Caught</u>
3. Spell: <u>Plenty</u>
4. Spell: <u>Breakfast</u>
5. Spell: <u>Weather</u>
6. Spell: <u>Health</u>
7. Spell: <u>Friend</u>
8. Spell: <u>Ground</u>
9. Spell: <u>Circle</u>
10. Spell: <u>City</u>
11. Spell: <u>Happy</u>
12. Spell: <u>Hurt</u>

Answers

Spelling 3-23

1. Spell: Heat
2. Spell: Valley
3. Spell: Easy
4. Spell: More
5. Spell: Instead
6. Spell: Somewhere
7. Spell: Everywhere
8. Spell: Getting
9. Spell: Island
10. Spell: Matter
11. Spell: Nobody
12. Spell: Invite

Spelling 3-24

1. Spell: Pretty
2. Spell: Here
3. Spell: Baby
4. Spell: Between
5. Spell: Someone
6. Spell: River
7. Spell: Wire
8. Spell: Sudden
9. Spell: Hour
10. Spell: Reach
11. Spell: Remember
12. Spell: Busy

Answers

Spelling 3-25

1. Spell: Piece
2. Spell: Whose
3. Spell: Perhaps
4. Spell: Potato
5. Spell: Tomato
6. Spell: Indeed
7. Spell: Child
8. Spell: Port
9. Spell: Plant
10. Spell: Bottom
11. Spell: March
12. Spell: Fruit

Spelling 3-26

1. Spell: Giant
2. Spell: Touch
3. Spell: Understand
4. Spell: Month
5. Spell: Wolf
6. Spell: Iron
7. Spell: Funny
8. Spell: Steady
9. Spell: Storm
10. Spell: Track
11. Spell: Most
12. Spell: Try

Answers

Spelling 3-27

1. Spell: Warm
2. Spell: Lion
3. Spell: Pear
4. Spell: Everything
5. Spell: Through
6. Spell: Always
7. Spell: Divide
8. Spell: Useful
9. Spell: Throat
10. Spell: Accident
11. Spell: Accidentally
12. Spell: Actual

Spelling 3-28

1. Spell: Actually
2. Spell: Address
3. Spell: Although
4. Spell: Answer
5. Spell: Appear
6. Spell: Arrive
7. Spell: Believe
8. Spell: Bicycle
9. Spell: Breath
10. Spell: Breathe
11. Spell: Build
12. Spell: Busy

Answers

Spelling 3-29

1. Spell: Business
2. Spell: Calendar
3. Spell: Caught
4. Spell: Center (US) Centre (UK)
5. Spell: Century
6. Spell: Certain
7. Spell: Complete
8. Spell: Consider
9. Spell: Continue
10. Spell: Decide
11. Spell: Describe
12. Spell: Different

Spelling 3-30

1. Spell: Difficult
2. Spell: Disappear
3. Spell: Eight
4. Spell: Eighth
5. Spell: Enough
6. Spell: Exercise
7. Spell: Experience
8. Spell: Experiment
9. Spell: Various
10. Spell: Extreme
11. Spell: Famous
12. Spell: Favorite (US) Favourite (UK)

Answers

Spelling 3-31

1. Spell: February
2. Spell: Forward
3. Spell: Forwards
4. Spell: Fruit
5. Spell: Grammar
6. Spell: Group
7. Spell: Guard
8. Spell: Guide
9. Spell: Heard
10. Spell: Heart
11. Spell: Heights
12. Spell: History

Spelling 3-32

1. Spell: Imagine
2. Spell: Increase
3. Spell: Important
4. Spell: Interest
5. Spell: Knowledge
6. Spell: Learn
7. Spell: Length
8. Spell: Library
9. Spell: Material
10. Spell: Medicine
11. Spell: Mention
12. Spell: Minute

Answers

Spelling 3-33

1. Spell: Natural
2. Spell: Notice
3. Spell: Occasion
4. Spell: Occasionally
5. Spell: Often
6. Spell: Opposite
7. Spell: Ordinary
8. Spell: Particular
9. Spell: Peculiar
10. Spell: Popular
11. Spell: Position
12. Spell: Possess

Spelling 3-34

1. Spell: Possession
2. Spell: Possible
3. Spell: Potatoes
4. Spell: Pressure
5. Spell: Probably
6. Spell: Promise
7. Spell: Purpose
8. Spell: Quarter
9. Spell: Question
10. Spell: Recent
11. Spell: Regular
12. Spell: Reign

Answers

Spelling 3-35

1. Spell: Remember
2. Spell: Sentence
3. Spell: Separate
4. Spell: Special
5. Spell: Straight
6. Spell: Strange
7. Spell: Strength
8. Spell: Suppose
9. Spell: Surprise
10. Spell: Therefore
11. Spell: Thought
12. Spell: Though

Spelling 3-36

1. Spell: Women
2. Spell: Slide
3. Spell: Swings
4. Spell: Admit
5. Spell: Regret
6. Spell: Property
7. Spell: Weight
8. Spell: Naughty
9. Spell: Type
10. Spell: Ache
11. Spell: Headache
12. Spell: Neglected

Other Books You'll Love!

1. **Spelling one: An Interactive Vocabulary & Spelling** Workbook for 5-Year-Olds. (With Audiobook Lessons)

2. **Spelling Two: An Interactive Vocabulary & Spelling** Workbook for 6-Year-Olds. (With Audiobook Lessons)

3. **Spelling Three: An Interactive Vocabulary & Spelling** Workbook for 7-Year-Olds. (With Audiobook Lessons)

4. **Spelling Four: An Interactive Vocabulary & Spelling** Workbook for 8-Year-Olds. (With Audiobook Lessons)

5. **Spelling Five: An Interactive Vocabulary & Spelling** Workbook for 9-Year-Olds. (With Audiobook Lessons)

6. **Spelling Six: An Interactive Vocabulary & Spelling** Workbook for 10 & 11 Years Old. (With Audiobook Lessons)

7. **Spelling Seven: An Interactive Vocabulary & Spelling** Workbook for 12-14 Years-Old. (With Audiobook Lessons)

Other Books You'll Love!

8. Raising Boys in Today's Digital World:
Proven Positive Parenting Tips for Raising Respectful, Successful, and Confident Boys

9. Raising Girls in Today's Digital World:
Proven Positive Parenting Tips for Raising Respectful, Successful, and Confident Girls

10. Raising Kids in Today's Digital World:
Proven Positive Parenting Tips for Raising Respectful, Successful, and Confident Kids

11. The Child Development and Positive Parenting Master Class 2-in-1 Bundle:
Proven Methods for Raising Well-Behaved and Intelligent Children, with Accelerated Learning Methods

12. Parenting Teens in Today's Challenging World 2-in-1 Bundle: Proven Methods for Improving Teenager's Behaviour with Positive Parenting and Family Communication

13. Life Strategies for Teenagers:
Positive Parenting, Tips and Understanding Teens for Better Communication and a Happy Family

14. Parenting Teen Girls in Today's Challenging World:
Proven Methods for Improving Teenager's Behaviour with Whole Brain Training

Other Books You'll Love!

15. **Parenting Teen Boys in Today's Challenging World:**
Proven Methods for Improving Teenager's Behaviour with Whole Brain Training

16. **101 Tips For Helping With Your Child's Learning**:
Proven Strategies for Accelerated Learning and Raising Smart Children Using Positive Parenting Skills

17. **101 Tips for Child Development:**
Proven Methods for Raising Children and Improving Kids Behavior with Whole Brain Training

18. **Financial Tips to Help Kids:**
Proven Methods for Teaching Kids Money Management and Financial Responsibility

19. **Healthy Habits for Kids:**
Positive Parenting Tips for Fun Kids Exercises, Healthy Snacks, and Improved Kids Nutrition

20. **Mini Habits for Happy Kids:**
Proven Parenting Tips for Positive Discipline and Improving Kids' Behavior

21. **Good Habits for Healthy Kids 2-in-1 Combo Pack**:
Proven Positive Parenting Tips for Improving Kid's Fitness and Children's Behavior

22. **Raising Teenagers to Choose Wisely:**
Keeping your Teen Secure in a Big World

23. **Tips for #CollegeLife:**
Powerful College Advice for Excelling as a College Freshman

Other Books You'll Love!

24. **The Career Success Formula:**
Proven Career Development Advice and Finding Rewarding Employment for Young Adults and College Graduates

25. **The Motivated Young Adult's Guide to Career Success and Adulthood:**
Proven Tips for Becoming a Mature Adult, Starting a Rewarding Career, and Finding Life Balance

26. **Bedtime Stories for Kids:**
Short Funny Stories and poems Collection for Children and Toddlers

27. **Guide for Boarding School Life**

28. **The Fear of The Lord:**
How God's Honour Guarantees Your Peace

Audiobooks
Are available at any of the following retailers:

1. Kobo
https://www.kobo.com/us/en/audiobook/spelling-three-1

2. Google Store
https://play.google.com/store/audiobooks/details/Bukky_Ekine_Ogunlana_Spelling_Three?id=AQAAAEAi-y27HM

3. Libro
https://libro.fm/audiobooks/9798368921990

4. Storytel
https://www.storytel.com/se/sv/books/4261927

5. Scribd
https://www.scribd.com/audiobook/637100286/Spelling-Three-An-Interactive-Vocabulary-and-Spelling-Workbook-for-7-Year-Olds-With-Audiobook-Lessons

6. Audiobooks
https://www.audiobooks.com/audiobook/spelling-three-an-interactive-vocabulary-and-spelling-workbook-for-7-year-olds-with-audiobook-lessons/680464

7. Barnes and Noble
https://www.barnesandnoble.com/w/spelling-three-bukky-ekine-ogunlana/1143328314

8. Spotify
https://open.spotify.com/show/65l4jsMvK2z9tbT8uU9S2X

9. Hoopladigital
https://www.hoopladigital.com/title/16139523

10. Chirpbooks
https://www.chirpbooks.com/audiobooks/spelling-three-by-bukky-ekine-ogunlana

And all other audiobook retailers!

Facebook Community

I invite you to our Facebook community group to visit this link and simply click the join group.

https://www.facebook.com/groups/397683731371863

This is a private group where parents, teachers, and carers can learn, share tips, ask questions, and discuss and get valuable content about raising and parenting modern children.

It is a very supportive and encouraging group where valuable content, free resources, and exciting discussion about parenting are shared. You can use this to benefit from social media.

You will learn a lot from schoolteachers, experts, counselors, and new and experienced parents, and stay updated with our latest releases.

See you there!

Your Free Gift

Your Free Gift!

As a way of saying thank you for Your purchase, I have included a gift that you can download at

TCEC publishing .com

References

1. https://www.theseus.fi/bitstream/handle/10024/50239/Anttila_Marianna_Saikkonen_Pinja.pdf
2. https://www.researchgate.net/publication/28372104_Early_Reading_Development
3. https://www2.ed.gov/parents/academic/help/adolescence/adolescence.pdf
4. http://centerforchildwelfare.org/kb/prprouthome/Helping%20Your%20Children%20Navigate%20Their%20Teenage%20Years.pdf
5. https://www.childrensmn.org/images/family_resource_pdf/027121.pdf
6. https://educationnorthwest.org/sites/default/files/developing-empathy-in-children-and-youth.pdf
7. https://www.researchgate.net/publication/263227023_Family_Time_Activities_and_Adolescents'_Emotional_Well-being
8. http://www.delmarlearning.com/companions/content/1418019224/AdditionalSupport/box11.1.pdf
9. https://exeter.anglican.org/wp-content/uploads/2014/11/Listening-to-children-leaflet_NCB.pdf
10. https://www.researchgate.net/publication/312600262_Creative_Thinking_among_Preschool_Children

www.ingramcontent.com/pod-product-compliance
Lightning Source LLC
Chambersburg PA
CBHW050416120526
44590CB00015B/1983